Hi! I'm Bori.
I was born in Jin-do, South Korea.
People call me Jindo dog.

I have fur as white as snow and floppy ears.
Everyone thinks Jindo dogs are so
handsome,
and I hope I'll be handsome, too.
Do you think I will be?

Now, I just play with my friends on this hill,
where I can see the turquoise sea in the
distance.
This place is so great.

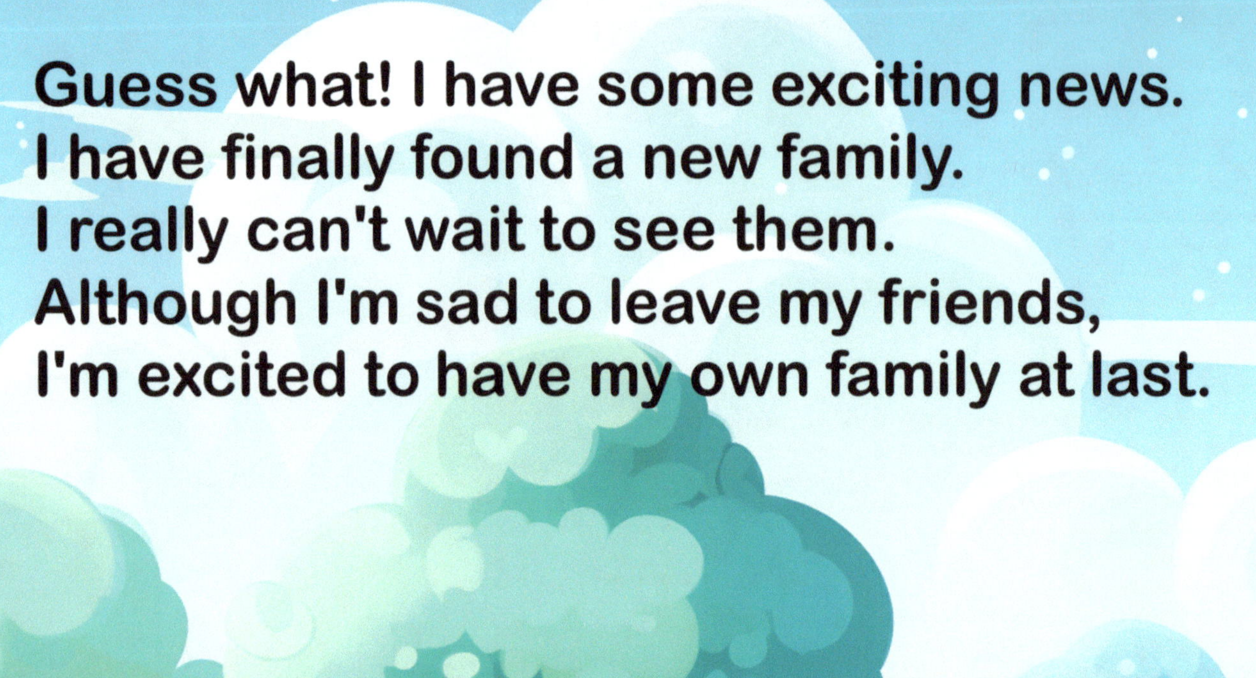

Guess what! I have some exciting news.
I have finally found a new family.
I really can't wait to see them.
Although I'm sad to leave my friends,
I'm excited to have my own family at last.

It looks like some people are coming over here to see me. They look like nice people.
How can I tell they're nice? Take a guess!
When I went up to them, they put their hands out to pet me.
I'm so thankful that they let me sniff their hands.
My tail is wagging with happiness.
Would you do the same thing?

This is my new home.
I love its big spacious yard.
I'm going to make this place my very own.
Jindo dogs have a strong sense of guarding their territory.
I will protect my family, too.

Even if a wild boar breaks into this house, I still won't be afraid.
When I grow up, I'll be so big and strong.

This is Jeong Min.
He's my new brother and my best friend.
He always plays with me and takes me for walks.
That's why he's my favorite.

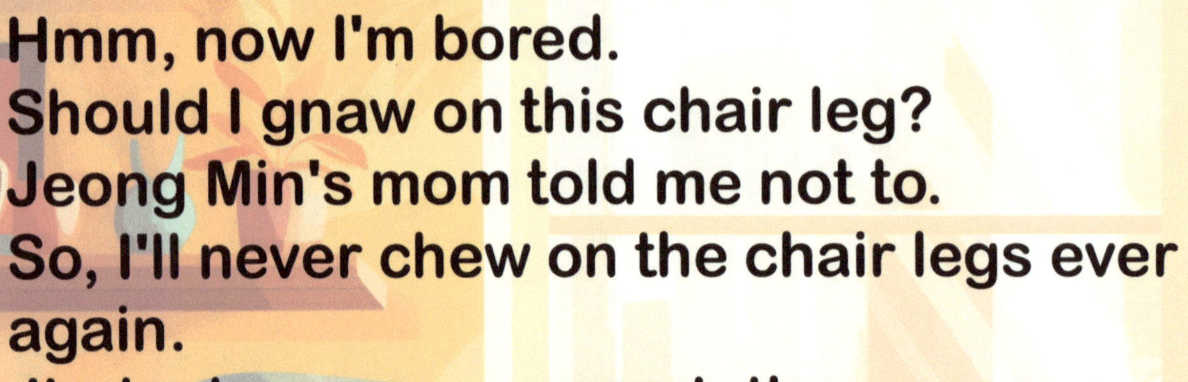

Hmm, now I'm bored.
Should I gnaw on this chair leg?
Jeong Min's mom told me not to.
So, I'll never chew on the chair legs ever again.
Jindo dogs are so smart, they can even understand what people say.

I love my new family so much.
Many Jindo dogs never forget their first owners.
To prove it, here's a well-known story.
Once, a Jindo dog was sold to a family that lived over 300 kilometers away.
But he missed his first owners so much that he ran away to go and find them.
He ran and ran for seven months, and finally he found his first home again.
Can you believe how smart and loyal he is?

I'm bored again, so I'm just sitting in the yard.
Jeong Min and his parents have gone away for the day.
Where did they go?
I'm all alone, playing with my toys.

Yay, Jeong Min is back!
Hmm, I smell something unfamiliar.
Jeong Min's dad has brought home a brand-new dog!
He's covered with lots and lots of fur.
He's a Sapsal dog, another native Korean dog.

Like his name suggests, he wards off bad luck.
Isn't that amazing?
We're friends now.

When Jindo dogs grow up by themselves,
they're more alert and focus on guarding
their home.
But if, when they're young, they meet lots of
different people and dogs,
they're a lot more likely to get along well
with others.

Wow, I've got some surprising news!
We are going to travel around the world!
My family saw how well I got along with the Sapsal dog.
So, they decided to take me to lots of different places and meet all kinds of new dogs.

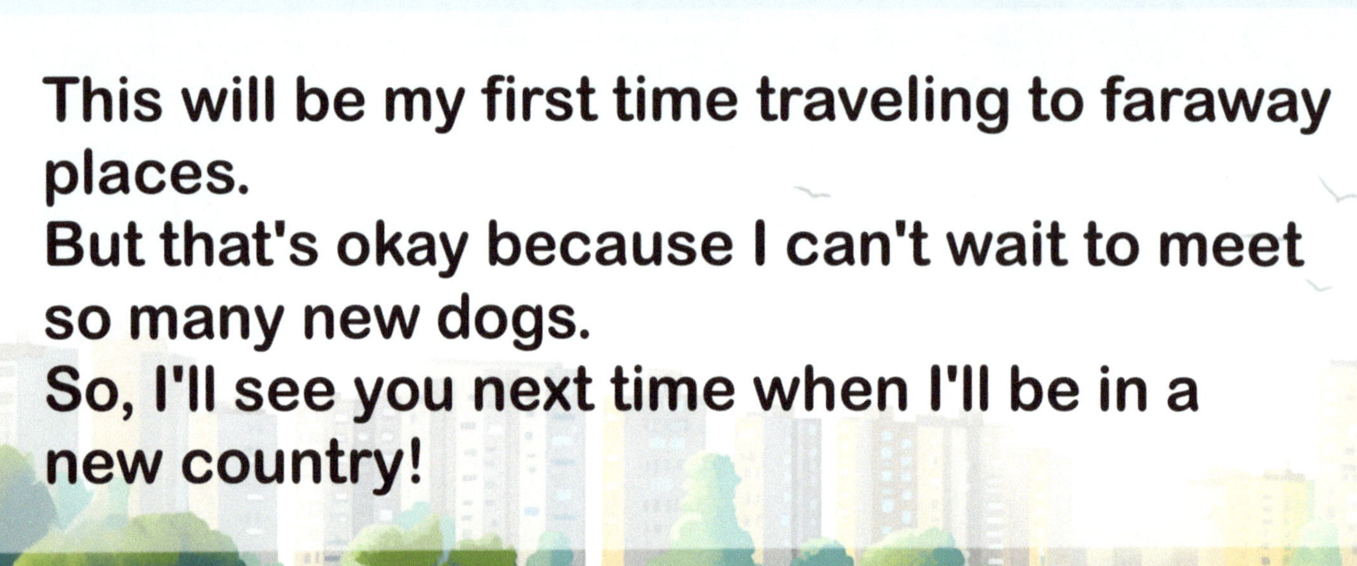

This will be my first time traveling to faraway places.
But that's okay because I can't wait to meet so many new dogs.
So, I'll see you next time when I'll be in a new country!